The Marrow of Longing

Celeste Nazeli Snowber

HARP Publishing
The People's Press
Clydesdale, Nova Scotia
Canada

HARP: The People's Press
216 Clydesdale Road
Clydesdale, Nova Scotia
Canada B2G 2K9

www.harppublishing.ca

Information about purchasing copies of this book can be
obtained from the publishers

harppeoplespress@gmail.com

tel. 902-863-0396

Catalogue-in-Publication data is on file with the Library and Archives Canada

ISBN: 978-1-990137-06-8

Cover and Interior paintings and drawings:
Marsha Nouritza Odabashian

Graphic design: Cathy Lin

Atken Armenian Foundation will receive 10% of all sales.
https://www.atkenarmenianfoundation.com

The Marrow of Longing

Celeste Nazeli Snowber

Celeste Snowber is a creative dynamo encompassing music and dance into her poetry in such a way that it echoes with a myriad of emotions reflecting like a mirror in which we can see our own heart and soul. *The Marrow of Longing* is a gentle generational walk down a highway of smiles and tears that weaves us into Snowber's blanket of lyric and dance that permeate the fabric of relationships and life. The words and emotions in this mix of free verse and prose poetry dance with eloquent ease to the surreal symphony they evoke in the reader's mind.

Candice James, Poet Laureate Emerita,
New Westminster, BC and author of *Rithimus Aeternam*

Harrowing, beautiful and surprising…through her exquisite capacity to listen, Celeste *shows us* person & place, land & love, all that is treasured beyond time, can be discovered within the living heart. It is clear to me that these poems are made with the soles of her bare feet, listening.

John Fox
The Healing Art of Poem-Making

I savored this volume with its carefully constructed fragments about identity, food and longing, all of them representations of love and wisdom. A morsel of joy.

Lola Koundakjian
Author of *The Moon in the Cusp of My Hand*

In this period of tremendous loss for the Armenian nation, it's good to see that our artists continue to so carefully share our complex and unresolved history through their personal journeys.

Atom Egoyan, Film Director, Writer, Producer

Celeste Snowber's *The Marrow of Longing* is a liminal site where land, food, bodysoul, the domestic, and the wild intermesh. These poems celebrate the succulent riches of Armenian cuisine in a tradition where food-making and artmaking are one, the kitchen a studio holding an eggplant's "plum black" richness. Readers are invited to open hearts and minds to the intergenerational traumas of the Armenian genocide of 1915 while stepping into a world where an Armenian mother's sweeping of floors sweeps us into an ever-present, enduring love.

Susan McCaslin, Author of *Into the Open: Poems New & Selected*

Here, held in the warm love of the familial kitchen and the embrace of earth longing, you can taste beneath the skin of black plum, experience sticky bursts of knowing dancing on your lips, and hear the grace in mother's admonishment of "Do it again, sweep the floor with love." Be swept into Snowber's embrace as she wraps you in voices, echoes and sighs, journeying us through heart and earth healings. While these poems share Snowber's cultural memory fragments, her words echo universal themes bringing us back to ourselves into the generational embodied cycle of mother, child, mother earth, child, repeating. We are reminded that love is created in making, through birthing, and Snowber generates love in the recursive process of helping us remember. Read and be reborn.

Pauline Sameshima, Canada Research Chair, Poet and Artist

All my longings lie open before you, Lord;
my sighing is not hidden from you.

Psalm 38:9

This book is dedicated to my mother
Grace Terzian Snowber
(1912-1986)

all my Armenian family

my three sons, Lucas, Caleb & Micah

and to my ancestors

Contents

Introduction

The Armenian soul is carved with absences. Longing for the land which was left. Longing for the mothers and sons, fathers and daughters, siblings and spouses who were killed and experienced atrocities. When I understood that the actual word *longing* is within *belonging*, I embraced longing as my greatest gift, a catalyst for growing the creative. Here is the desire to create and to live in the in-between of the already and not yet. In this liminal space, I am called to write and dance. My pilgrimage into my heritage is a journey to discover the poetic as a site from which the primordial lives. Here is a place where intergenerational trauma is transformed through art.

The Marrow of Longing is a collection of poems that traverses the journey of being raised by an artistic mother who survived the Armenian genocide. They are forged out of my voracious desire to integrate my Armenian identity in my life—both the beauty and horror. The beauty of a rich heritage of an ancient civilization that breathes within my bones. The horror of the genocide of 1.5 million Armenians killed and the victims of horrific and unspeakable acts against humanity. These poetic words are other acts, acts that are speakable, and finding voice.

Paradoxes dwell together in this terrain and it is taking me a lifetime to parse their meaning and recover the potency of fragments. I am continually cognizant that I am formed, informed and transformed by my cultural background. We are storied people, and found in each other's stories. What happens to one happens to many.

Longing is integral to my life. The marrow of these poems explore place, identity, longing and belonging. The juxtapositions of the holy and the ordinary, beauty, difficulty, and absurdity are best articulated through the poetic. From cooking to colour to the art of worrying, or how longing infuses a life are the staples of these poems. I trace the ache of the heart, the yearnings of the body. The reverberations of memory and trauma crack open ways to live artistically. The fragments, which find their way in poems, become a way to excavate the terroir of my Armenian culture; both in the diaspora as well as my ancestral history.

Many of these poems have been danced and performed and here they are woven into a collection of poetic utterances. Mother and daughter and mother and sons thread through the *Marrow of Longing*. Fifty-four fragments explore the relationships between land, food, the body and love from one generation to the next.

My mother Grace was born in Kharpert in historic Armenia, and came to the Boston area as a child and my father, Frank was born in Brooklyn of primarily Irish descent. My parents comprised my whole immediate family as an only child. They left the world early, just as I started my third decade, they died eight months from each other. I started a new family and yet what impacted me over the years is how the nature of presence can be found in absence. They were with me in spirit during the years I raised my three children even though they never met them in the flesh.

All I am left are fragments to piece a cultural heritage.
Fragments can contain the whole. Just as a sample of DNA
points to origins, words break open understanding.
I search for fragments as collecting precious sea glass.

This collection is an intimate window to how biography
and history has shaped and reshapes me. My hope is that
Marrow of Longing can be a space for you to honour and
discover what has shaped your own life.

Here I offer fragments, and a fragment can hold a world.

kitchen & colour

I

Kitchen Studio   *Marsha Nouritza Odabashian*

When I cook Armenian food, I bring my mother to the table;
smells inhabit my home
foods that formed me first
and then my three sons.
Identity and place are wed in food. If we are fortunate enough
to have food baked into ethnicity, we can arrive again and again
to aromas of childhood
the recipes hidden in the body.

There is also food for the soul.
Absences are present in the yearning
for forgotten stories, for the ones who died before I was born
for grandparents and great-grandparents,
for family killed in the genocide
for questions one never asked of a parent.
For the stories from generations ago.

What happens when whole villages are wiped out?

I have only fragments of memory
I discover handwritten pieces on parchment,
letters my mother wrote to my father in World War II.

Stories are born in kitchens.
Fragments of food, fragments of life.

Beneath the Skin of Plum Black

Aromas took second place
to hues of dark purple
it was your colours
my mother was
in love with.

Eggplant.
Jeweled in sautéed onions
adorned with red
pepper, a hint
of green parsley
a slice of lamb.

Plum black
you are love marinated
in drips of oil
tenderized in
the h/earth
in a New England kitchen.

Star leaves
at slender head
pear like in shape
endless dishes
meals of everyday
formed from you
smooth to fingers touch
a sacred vegetable
in its nakedness.

I've disguised
you for my children's palate
mushed you with olive oil,
yogurt and plenty of garlic

transformed you into
babaganoosh, still
a far cry from
101 ways my mother
would lovingly open
you up to your
pungent parts.

Never leave the pan without
a hint of green, she said,
Look how stunning the red
pepper accents blackened violet.

In the pan—
smells, textures, hues
were the heavens of the
new earth, and the
scent of the old land.

Second-generation creativity
close to the bone
colour is the heart
of my home
hidden in the eggplant
and hidden in a life.

My mother had an
eggplant soul
a beauty of both
dark and light
rough and tender
yellow white flesh
encased in mauves
the meeting of art and life
just beneath the
skin of plum black.

Swept in Her Love

Sweep the kitchen floor one more time,
she said.

It was a chore
I wanted to finish fast

her Boston accent resounding
Do it again,
Sweep the floor with love.

When I finally visit Yerevan
every dawn the streets are graced
with feet and arms sweeping
sidewalks and storefronts
sounds that wake daylight.

Mamma's voice
echoes
here on these streets.

Once again—
swept in her love.

Morning Aromatics

the placement of herbs alone
is an art form
      every shape of p
               a
               r
               s
               l
               e
               y

curly, root and flat leaf
rosette of tripinnate leaves
      dill and cilantro
onion and purple basil
      adorn the market
a sculpture of herbaceous plants
        hues of mint, lime, moss
        jade, emerald, burgundy
haunt me to ancestral greens
of Eastern Anatolia.

I eat breakfast
in my modest room in Armenia

madzoon and a panoply of fresh herbs
laid out
      morning's aromatics
food group unto themselves.

In Praise of the Kitchen-Studio

She made paper roses
sold them on the street
in Cambridge, Massachusetts
brought reapings to her family at eleven.

She escaped the aftermath
the heart does not cease
to know the lament
of the forefathers and foremothers
from the old country.

The year before her death at seventy-three
she still brought flowers to life
even after my father died
arranging living anthurium
petals into modern art.

My mother's kitchen was an art studio
cooking with colour
creating flower arrangements
with metals, plexiglass
driftwood and plant life.

In my kitchen
I knock out a wall
put in a wooden floor
my dance studio
is where I cook
and always, always
there will be flowers.

I am made and re-made
in my kitchen studio.

Recipes in the Body

She cooked through her body
an intuitive scent in the fingers
a little of this, a dash of that
they knew just the right amount.

There was no cookbook
in the old country
food was a dialect they spoke
to cook for those you love
the recipe is passed down
from tongue to tongue
heart to tongue.

I long for aromas
flavours of my childhood
every Christmas I make cheese boureg
I am closer to the tastes I remember
cheese melts in a mouth with parsley
I still don't make it like my mother.

I revisit my childhood
eat at my friend Ari's family home
his Armenian mother and grandmother release
tastes and textures of my youth—
pine nuts and lamb, green beans and tomato
caressed in olive oil, dolma stuffed with filling.

I cannot stop thinking of
explosions on my palate
I dream of every food
in my household growing up that was stuffed
meatballs, peppers, tomatoes, and grapeleaves
I lament that my children
haven't eaten anything stuffed
except a bird.

Recipes
hidden in the body
stored in memory and marrow
wait to be taken
into the stew of my life.

Lavash Wisdom

for Serge & Anush at Lamajuoun ~ The Armenian Bakery
of BC

He tells me of his grandmother's wisdom
the dough needs to be as soft
as the touch of his ear lobe
but it is really her ear
that the softness of the lavash
was measured by.

The bakers here bring lamajoun, gata, fresh lavash,
basturma, sujuk, and Armenian jingalov bread
with natural ingredients—
smells intoxicate me upon entrance

Love is the source.

This Christmas

    after three decades in Vancouver

I enter for the first time
an Armenian bakery

    suddenly my mother is before me
    with her weathered hands
    in the markets in Watertown,
    Massachusetts.

A nation is found in one bite.

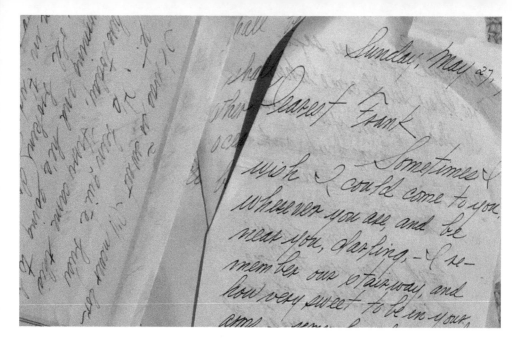

Fragments

To piece my heritage
shards of genocide
a thousand stained glass pieces
of wounds and wombs
shimmer and illuminate.

My mom told me about her dad Mesrop
He told her, *knowledge is an invisible*
gold bracelet on your wrist.

My task:
to listen to fragmentia
live my life
in the poetics of parts.

I want to wear
fragments as bracelets
let the invisible
adorn me.

Fragments of My Mother's Letters

I

Outside my grandmother's kitchen window—

Mt. Ararat.

As she grew up
my mom grew up longing for what she did
not get to see

Before I die
I shall see the snow-capped peaks
of Mt. Ararat at whose distance
I came into the world.
Life will be a full circle
an invisible mandala.

II.

She speaks of dance—

Jan Veen thinks I can
be in his new ballet
I take free classes.

I also took classes from Shumita
Hindu dance and La Meri
hours of rehearsals
Here I come alive
when I dance.

III.

I make all the clothes
for my family
work at Westinghouse
and Cox Engineering
as a secretary
to support my family.

Notes: Jan Veen and La Meri were pioneers in dance
history, Jan Veen for bringing ballet and modern dance to
Boston and La Meri for bringing ethnic dance to the West.

Passage

for my grandfather Mesrop

I never met my grandfather Mesrop Terzian, born in 1877,
in Kharpert, historic Armenia.
I piece remains and stitch threads from remnants.

You sat at the kitchen table with my mom and drew pictures
of the Armenian plateau hills where you played your flute,
tended sheep on the land. You told stories of being a goat
herder in the countryside. You were well acquainted with
poets & writers of Armenia and shared them with my mom.

She tells me, *My father was the only one who could relate
to me in an aesthetic sense.* You also told her, *If you seek
knowledge you will never be poor.*

She was your eldest. You taught them all how to read and
write Armenian. If any of the kids wanted anything, they
first had to write the request in Armenian.

You sold your family's jewelry to help pay for passage to the
United States. You came in steerage on the *SS Oceania* with
your wife Aghavni and daughter Grace sailed from Patras,
Greece and arrived in Ellis Island, New York in 1913. You
settled in Cambridge, Massachusetts and had four other
children: John, Paul, Mary and Carney; my aunt and
uncles. Your mother's name was Nazeli, my middle name,
your father's name Boghos. You changed your name from
Tertzagian to Terzian and you were hard working and had a
temper. You died of a heart attack in 1940. You were

drilling the street with a jackhammer in Boston. You left behind a wife of 48 years, and five children aged 28, 27, 24, 22, 14.

What remains are your children and grandchildren.

The Story of One

If we only have fragments
aren't all our pieces a whole?

what happens to one
happens to all

so much has gone missing
strands of DNA
whisper a mystery

the story of one
is the survival of a nation.

Tricentennial, 1976 (Interpreting Light Year 2076)
Grace Terzian Snowber

Where is the Lexicon of Women Artists?

for my mother Grace

Women were excluded from the canon.

She was ahead of her time, gave me the treatise, *Concerning the Spiritual in Art* by the expressionist Wassily Kandinsky. At the early age of five she brings me to the Guggenheim Museum in NYC, weeps in front of "Improvisation 28,"where I have my first art history lesson—aesthetics of color has hidden meaning. Her artistic companions were dead; male painters and philosophers and then there was Jesus, who lived in her heart.

She shows me the artist Robert Delaunay's work where geometric shapes and hues were everything. She took the abstract principles into her creations and paintings, let the shapes and curves seep into her limbs. Her flower arrangements became sculptures, welding materials in flight—one red amaryllis pressed between driftwood and metal reaching upward, not the average floral composition for the local community garden club in New England.

I recall her tales of sitting on Newbury Street during her lunch hour in Back Bay of Boston in the 1940s, having coffee with a group of international artists, who later became acclaimed and remarkable icons to the world. They would also come to her mother's and my grandma's kitchen.

Armenian composer Alan Hovhaness
Hyman Bloom the Latvian-American painter
Ravi Shankar, the well-known Indian musician

What if she had been granted the same opportunities as her
male counterparts?
Where is the lexicon of women immigrant artists in the
United States during this time?
The women were held down with domestic duties of
survival. My mom supported her family as a secretary, but
always had fire and flora in her heart.
Eventually she created art, wherever she stepped, danced,
painted, arranged flowers and cooked in coming decades.

Her vibrancy still courses through my veins.

Stained Glass Love

She carefully planned
each colour of hand blown glass
juxtaposed geometric contours
where island light
could enter

Stains of blue, lavender, burnt orange
ochre, mauve, and mint green
lead in between metallic
gold hues on antique glass
graced our living room windows
overlooking the grey blue Atlantic

I spent hours gazing
at the shades of light
the evening illuminations

Long after she is gone
glass traps light
in shapes and shades
of precious shards
that still shatter hearts.

Remnants

A few remnants remain
after I cleaned out the closet
when she died. A brown
chestnut velvet dress
cut to fitted waist, knee length
stylish form in the 1940s
buttons were an art form
lined down the back,
I never fit its tapered curves.

Her talent in sewing
did not translate; I never
got the waistband and zipper
precise on the first skirt I made
in seventh grade home-economics class.

I treasure the photos
of the beautiful shirt she made
when I was in second grade
peach, pink, yellow and cream
bright as daffodils in our yard
hung on my little frame.

If she made all the clothes
for her siblings, who taught her?
her maiden name Terzian
comes from *terzi* meaning tailor.
precision and craft made visible
in the garments of her siblings.

Dressed with care
only a daughter knows
decades later.

Pockets, Peanuts and Raisins

Food was a constant subject
in my home growing up
Don't forget the starving Armenians!
my mother said in a Boston accent, all the r's dropped
sta'ving Armenians, with all the emotion
gutturals in her throat
shaking through the body.

Pockets, peanuts & raisins in her dress
first-grade little Gracie sent off
to school in Porter Square near
Harvard Square in Cambridge
redheaded girl being loaded
up with peanuts & raisins
in her left and right pockets
she told me the tale repeatedly.

The teacher chastises her
for not bringing some for the whole class
she returns home
her mother worried
her daughter might be hungry.

Years later I got it
reading the horrifying accounts
of millions of Armenians
marched out to the Syrian Desert to starve
those who survived and escaped
had hunger as a constant companion.

The peanuts & raisins of survival
food in the pocket
at one's fingertips
P & R was always scattered through my home
small bowls everywhere
before the onset of allergies

Today I carry sunflower seeds
almonds and dried cranberries
everywhere I go.

The Food for Life
for Patsy Heath

Two women in Save-On-Foods in the line-up
waiting to pay for their groceries
recognize one another
we come from the same origins.

I carry a book of Peter Balakian's poems
she turns and asks if I'm Armenian
I've lived in Vancouver for over twenty years
and never met an Armenian
longing is not an item I need to purchase.

Our chance meeting grows into a long deep friendship
Patsy and I uncover fragments of our herstories.

Two hundred miles apart from each other
her parents from Erzurum,
my mother and grandparents from Kharpert
both places and their peoples violently destroyed.

Texture of loss
our ancestors who survived
could not voice the unspeakable grief.

Make new lives here
mine in Cambridge, Massachusetts of the U.S.
hers in Burnaby, British Columbia of Canada.

Today our families
would have been a five-hour drive from one another
we gather them in our hearts and sinews
ones we knew and loved
ones we never met.

Her body and my body remember together
here is the food of life
we pay for our groceries.

I give gratitude for heart connections
a friendship which goes beyond land and time
love that reaches back and moves forward

Here is the food for life.

Fig Sunday

Oh, Fig with your longest history on earth

      your unisex flowers
      I need more of you

I grew up on dried figs

      now I want you raw
      right off the tree, so I can place

you on everything from salads to salmon

Your hues change

      from golden to brown to resplendent
      purple; your hollow flesh, complex inflorescence

This is what I crave on a Sunday morning.

An Anatomy of a Pomegranate

Your names roll off my tongue
the beads of pomegranate
I keep repeating
    Arakel & Khatchkhatoun

translations speak into absence
    Arakel means *to send*
    Khatchkhatoun means *given by the cross*

You came from Kharpert
the Golden Plain of historic Armenia
parents of my grandmother
you are two of the one and a half million
killed in the genocide

each name a kernel
in my throat
names and membranes
seeds of mystery
ruby red held
in my pomegranate heart.

Batchig and Geragoor

I remember two words

> *batchig*: to kiss
> *geragoor*: food or meal

my mother reminds me
of these partners
in the every day

kissing the food
food as kiss

she left me
with what was necessary

earth & longing

II

Love in the Ruins   *Marsha Nouritza Odabashian*

My limbs, feet and torso beckon me through movement
to trace my beginnings.
I do not have family in Armenia.
I walk the land, allow my body to respond.

Stones hold memory
the ancient place becomes a site to birth
poetry and dance. I need to continue to uncover
my own history and embrace my longing.
In our collective narratives
we become known.

This is the work I do.
Listen to the rumblings
of my bodysoul.
Find the mystery which informs
living, being
transforming.

The Marrow of Longing

Longing resides in my marrow
a land inside my chest
asks to be familiar
a place I know belongs
to my longing.

She spoke of this land
over and over
tales of leaving as a baby
as if time had passed and she was ten, then twenty
yearning for a land was bred in my mother
her parents ached for the Armenia
they left, even the beauty of Cambridge
could not equal what was in their cells
that was the bread my mother was fed.

The body knows roots
soles of feet are souls
knowing earth
I am a child raised between land and sea
borders between is where I find home
an ache reaches
the earth in my body
my body in the earth.

Longing is the land I dwell.

Stone to Stone

I am letting you
wash over me Armenia
stone to stone
khachkar to khachkar
lavash to lavash

I cross thousands of miles
come home to your spring
ancient and green
dance my olive skin
on your baptized land.

Until You Touch

A fellow traveller said,

> *perhaps until you physically touch*
> *a thousand places on the land you will not*
> *find your roots.*

And this is what I know:
　　　the curve of stone
　　　smell of earth
　　　sounds of birds
　　　taste of lavash
　　　the gesture of dancing hands
　　　to feel the place I know
Within.

To touch soma
the memories creation
carries.

Palpable.
the land holds a truth
bears the scars and likes of loss
a thousand times.

Your Stones Wait

at Geghard Monastery

Space greets the holy
within your medieval walls
emptiness becomes a vessel
made to crack me open

I'm wooed to your womb
carved from mountain
cut from rock of the Azat valley

I dance ever so slowly
light pours through arches
remnants of dark frescoes

A force moves my spirit
limbs reach into the invisible.

Janoy, I Am Listening

Notes haunt me
knowing deeper than bone
from mater to matter
my mother's matrilineal line

where melodies alone
make sense to yearning
I forget reasons, maps, logic or time.

I recognize myself in *a cappella*
return home to atonal chords
conjugate a love song

where I listen.

Earth Traces

Geography holds

its own

      story—

hidden in scents

      of mud and sky

      flatbread and tears

ripen.

Eat

      the earth's song

hear

      its loud lament.

Villagers   *Marsha Nouritza Odabashian*

Ancestral Tones

We are not only
ones who died in the genocide
victims of horror

We are beauty incarnate
weavers, shoemakers, mothers & daughters
duduk players, poets, fathers & sons
priests, goat herders, scholars, silversmiths
brothers & sisters, bakers and artisans

and most of all—
We are land
baked from the terroir
of arid and fertile soil
figs, pomegranates, nettles and olives

Do not forget who we were
how we loved—
                    a poetic memoir of Armenians

We are notes on a tetrachord
calling forth polyphonic
in our bones
                    we are ancestral tones.

Olive Wisdom

The neighbors told her—

Olive trees can't grow here
not in the yard where we made home
        in a little island town named Nahant
on the Atlantic coast outside Boston

They thrive on Mediterranean climates
rocky soils well drained
        long hot summers
spring delivers leaves scattered like scars

We lived in the cold of New England
my mother the resilient weather
        unpredictable and persistent as Northeasters
pushing and rattling our windows

Our olive tree grew and grew
years after my mother died, a good decade
        until the new owners cut it down
in lieu of a lawn

My mother and the olive tree are gone
they both keep reminding me
        to dare to dream the impossible

Grow that olive tree
        that papaya, that hair, that idea
        that book, that life, that patio garden

Say YES to olive wisdom.

Seaweed Torment

I dive deep into the seaweed
of my own torment
        a child of twelve
        a mother of fifty-five

screams of rage
into salted air
of the gasping sea
kitchen turned abyss
cooked to turmoil.

How does a girl comprehend
this quick bend to chaos
love changed in an instant
to inconsolable rage?

I took to escaping
to a neighbors house
till her yelling died down

no one could love me like her
or live with so much colour and joy
all in the same woman, my mamma

Could art alone heal?
It didn't save Anne Sexton or Virginia Woolf
or the Armenian musician Gomidas.
she aged too fast
amidst a stroke and heart attacks

What if she could have kept creating
flower arrangements and paintings
danced by the sea?

I am now fifty-five, the age she was when
I was twelve; the pain body
surfaces and I am sometimes twelve
and all the ages in-between
love and scars.

Sea Glass Friends
for Patty Gregory

Ocean is our teacher
Maolis road hugs the curve
rocks grip the rugged coast
in front of both our houses
of an island town,
summers daily arrivals

We live on opposite coasts now
sustain our childhood passion
picking sea glass

I never tire of greens, amber, cream
occasional cobalt blue or lavender
weathered glass to archive
crop of ocean's edge

Each morning, I return to the shore
reap a new harvest from night's tussle

Long friendship and sea glass
two treasures in the salt of life
we gather sea treasures
on different shores
one Atlantic, one Pacific
two mothers of Armenian descent
two fathers of Irish descent

Our sea glass endures.

Vowels of the Body

I am more
of the earth
than I understand
floods of water
        ashes of fire

Seasons enter my flesh
internal tides, external rhythms
rain, mist, flames, ice
hormones

The language of moon
syllables of the tides
        navigate my body

Feel the voice of wind
        through sinews
        light in tissues
arc my backbone to being

I am more of this earth
than I understand.

Diaspora Dreams

I was never taught
the vowels, syllables of her native tongue
my mother held the shame
of being an immigrant.

Sixty-two years later
I grieve
what resonates and vibrates inside

I cannot ask—
       how to make cheese boureg
           the stories her mother knew
               how words roll in her mouth
                  how her dialect tastes.

Once dear uncle Carney
taught me the alphabet
as we sat at the kitchen table
as she stuffed grape leaves
the letters just marks
veins on the page
I still long for the sounds
of her ancient terrain.

Ripe with my history
longing for the alphabet
spoken against my skin.

An Alphabet of Longing

There are not enough letters
in the alphabet to define longing

the Armenian soul is
varied and complex
as the cuisine of food

aromas of sounds
the taste of words
inexpressible haunts

in the steps of migration.

Wisdom of Origins

No photo produces
what's lined in the tissues
scribed in cellular memory

Fragments last
the tide of time
longing present within

Ingredients are in the synapses
the taste of pilaf
the smell of yalanchee
crunch of tourshi, pickled vegetables
linger in the senses

A long conversation.

One Dancing Heart to Another

for Ruzan Vardanyan
and Antoine Terjanian

She longed for the monasteries
ancient in stone, engraved
from the love of God
a country she never saw again

She left as a child in 1913.

I travel all over Armenia
I enter this village in Yeghegnadzor
greeted by a troupe of dancers on a dirt road
a woman carries bread, radiates joy
adorned in Armenian costume
we recognize each other
one dancing heart to another

We dance the Kochari
see and taste lavash bread
baked from ovens in the ground
mountains surround us
home becomes a little closer

Here are my origins
a time I do not know
but have been aching for.

Birdsong Lessons

What do the birds teach us
in these times of pandemic?

Their music greets dawn
in a universal language
tweets, cackles, trills, pecks
vocalizing prayers
monovocal melodies of song sparrows
pitch, tempo, beats and whistles
vibrato of feathers, buzz of warblers

Tones of plumage
dialects beyond boundaries
winged iconography asks
what we feed on

Swallows forage in the sky
manna from the heavens

I come from a lineage of resilience
sustenance comes from above
inspires steps to move forward
become birdsong.

Voices Must Not Vanish

for Alan Whitehorn

Prophets, poets & scholars
call us to remembering

What is lost is returned
what is broken is an opening
Armenia woven in my fibres and tissues

Each grief is part of our grief
recognize what is not recognized
tell it again and again

Ancestries missing
villages and cities wiped out
names changed forever
survivors did not often share
the horrors.

Remember what is lost
Open what is broken
Write what is whole.

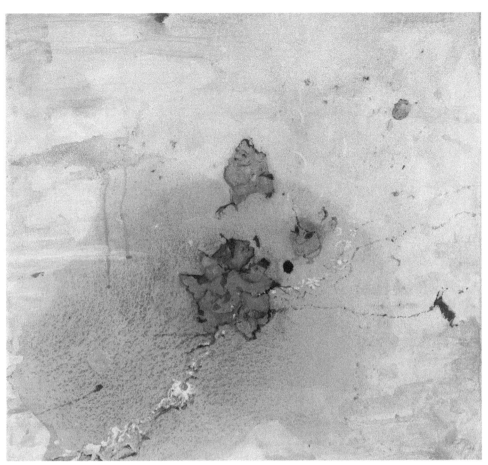

Milky Way Waltz   *Marsha Nouritza Odabashian*

Dissolving All Boundaries

on the other side
      of what cannot be seen
      constellations

turquoise galaxies gulp
      bodies
bones blast to sand
      swirling

borderlines
      where skin meets sky

cries out for a third way.

65

worry & spirituality

III

Arbor   *Marsha Nouritza Odabashian*

Connections between the holy and ordinary
have long held my fascination
How prayer is infused in the act of worrying,
how cooking a beautiful meal is an expression of the sacred,
how breath, ocean and awe connect.

The ordinary is a canvas of the holy.
Mothering and teaching are inseparable
from my dancing and swimming, walking and ruminating.
My life has never afforded hours for reflection,
so the examined life happens within the practices of daily living.
The mystery of life interweaves with the mundane.
We become wide-awake through all that is presented to us.
Vulnerabilities are a strength.
Fragility can be an awakening.
Poetry can be a transport.
We are in a state of yearning and becoming.
The richness in Armenian heritage
whether it is within illuminated manuscripts
stones of khatchkars or a soul of perseverance
opens the human soul to more.

In the cracks of life
lies the crucible
of the divine.

To Pray Is To Sigh

Tend children through the fragile night
with countless prayers.

Release whatever might hold them—

        generational bloodlines
        wounds that refuse to heal.

Prayer is beyond counting
there is no calculation
for how we carry those we love.

In the incense
the alchemy of transformation

To pray is to sigh—

        the leavening of love
        we throw past
        and beyond borders.

Transport

Let poetry be the transport
to the world beneath the words
where new words are born
amidst the volcanic ash
or the sweetness of choereg
cooked and eaten with love.

A passage exists
to the hymns of your heart
in a time of limitation
Mkrtich Naghash, 15th century poet priest said,
we are all exiles.

Take courage from the lineage
poetic steeped in the Armenian soul
proverbs, odes, love songs, lullabies
chants, folk tales, poems, laments—
a pilgrimage to what calls us
to the alphabet of yearning.

Be your own bard
migrate to the life waiting for you
Naghash says, *an exile's heart is tender.*

May the poet within you
in the silence of dawn
carry you over to tenderness.

Imposter

A stranger at the Armenian bakery stops me
when he notices how much lamajun I buy
He asks, *Are you Armenian?* I say, *YES, my
mother was born there.*
He asks, *Do you speak the language?* I yelled, *no.
Then you're NOT Armenian.*

I didn't go to Armenian school
I don't know the language
I'm only one/half Armenian

Sometimes I feel like an imposter

My Armenian mother made sure
that one-half is one hundred percent
every day she pointed to Mt. Ararat

I don't go to the Armenian church
I am a Christian feminist
seminary trained and love God

How can I be part of male leadership
endorse what I know not to be true?

      Even Jesus appeared to a woman first
      and proclaimed the urgency

Go tell them, *I have risen!*

Another language breathes through lungs
      vibrates in vocal folds

The linguistics of blood and bone
      a grammar deeper than the ear can hear.

Blood Lessons   *Marsha Nouritza Odabashian*

Blood Lessons

Traits passed down
from generation to generation—

Propensity for humour

heart disease

high blood pressure

a knack for telling stories

The way my hair waves
my desire to paint
the way I move my hips
or whether I like Labrador dogs
Inheritances—
how we care and be in life
how we hold the ache
for sons and daughters
sing hymns for the unborn

visions

dreams

plans

Stumble into
blood lessons.

Passion and Perseverance

for my sons: Lucas, Caleb and Micah

You are more Armenian
than you know
beloved three sons
never met my mother
or had the food she cooked

I've never made
       it as she did
       the boureg still doesn't come out
       just like hers
       you all loved it nonetheless.

Who can deny melted cheese?

You eat passion like boureg
yearning imbues your hearts.

What grandmothers and grandfathers
would never see continue
to sing beyond time.

Ode to Khachkars

Oh, cross-stones, chiseled with
vegetal designs and lace patterns
intricately carved in volcanic basalt

On your face, a cross intersects the world
sprouts in every direction
through leaves, grapes, tendrils
and always pomegranates

Your symmetry is ceremony.

Set in different parts of the country
from as early as the 9th century
you could have been erected for salvation
of soul, living or deceased
speak over tombs and memorials

You invite commemoration.

The first time I saw you in Armenia
erect outside of monasteries
sun and weather made you resplendent
only in fragments of green limestone

And I loved you more.

No two of you are alike
50,000 of you still live*
inscribed in the depths of our beings
we *are* living khachkars.

You are your own poems.

* Khachkars are on the UNESCO List of Intangible Cultural Heritage.

Whisper to Me Once More

Divine scent
cannot be contained
in any box
ritual, candle or cross

You leap off a cross
go through the body
unmeasured and luminous

Rumble through veins
poured in the blood
reverberate in water

You *are*
beyond and within
canticle of light
canticle of body
tongues of embers
rain to the synapses
fire in the solar plexus
this is the present.

Worry

Do you have your hat on?
what was your grade on your test?
did you do better than her?
did you turn off the lights?
what about the heat?
  was it turned down?
did the bills get paid?
is the chicken defrosting?
was there enough colour in
        sautéed peppers, dress, or painting
        or your cover on your schoolbooks?

Did you remember?
        The Turks killed the Armenians

Remember. Remember. Remember.

REMEMBER was a big VERB in my house growing up.

My Armenian mother said,
I might not have been able to have you
I finally conceived and bore you
You are my star of miracles

We are all miracles—
here,
forgotten, not born, killed or bled.

Worried for love.

Mater/Matter/Mother

After 20 years in therapy

      I realize

I am just Armenian

      Time is better spent

searching

      for my roots.

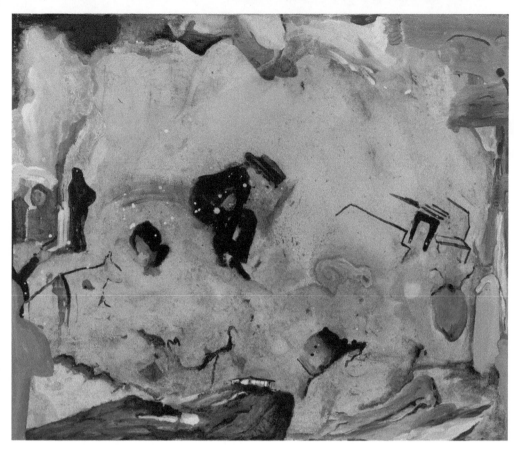

Guardians of Our Inheritance   *Marsha Nouritza Odabashian*

Privilege on My Ancestors' Backs

My privilege is on the backs
of those who suffered greatly
who experienced massacres
those who fled before the big one—
the full-fledged genocide
of the Armenians in 1915.

My privilege is on the backs
of those who worked so hard
they too had dreams
my grandparents never got to see
parents or family again, or
the country that they loved
they never went to college; nor did my
talented artistic mother,
still she created art.

My privilege is on the back
of my immigrant mother
coming to America as a
baby from Kharpert
carrying the hardship of two lands.

What is still inside
is in my own DNA, denial
reverberates when injustice is present
is on repeat, a never ending story
stand and walk in solidarity
with all who are discriminated
against, beaten in soul and flesh
bodies taken too soon.

My privilege comes on the back of love
for a new beginning, my parents and
ancestors all yearning for beginnings

Pressing on in the truth
that each life matters
each breath a gift.

Water Litany

It was the colours
        that bent her body
        towards the earth
        a prayer
        to the sea
        tiny opalescent gems
        gleamed through mud
        pebbles, twigs and shells
        shaded green weeds of sea

        rhythm of bending
        reaching and picking
gathering and releasing
placing and holding
in pockets—
tiny jewels of the sea
formed in the tango
between wind and tides
        she too was shaped
        by gusts, wind and oceans
        woman of seascapes

        this one gesture
        arms and shoulders
        hips and pelvis leaning

close to earth
        a litany to water,
        hands in
        sand and salt
sea glass and mud

she dropped down
where timelessness and
grace entwine
to inhabit her past—
fluidity, bypass the
shards of her own scars
luminous.

Parchment Love

They lived in the bureau
behind all her sweaters.

Her love was written
on the skin of paper
markings
ink of the heart.

I inherited them after
my mom and dad died
these love letters my mother
wrote to my father
in World War II
he was a merchant marine
visiting thirty-three countries
she wrote to him from outside Boston.

I refound them
just when I most needed them
my longing bigger than memory
mending fragments
snippets of her life as a younger woman
studying Hindu dance, painting in oils,
missing pieces of passion

From Grace to Frank ~
> *I love you, I love you, I love you*
> *It makes me pure and beautiful inside,*
> *It makes trees, trees, and sky, sky.*
> *It makes all things living.*
> *It brings the nearness of heaven.*

Through this love
I'm brought back.

Chants in the Old Chevy

I'm lying in the back seat
of the turquoise poly-green Chevy
sprawled across vinyl upholstery
in a no-seat-belt era
I'm singing and humming sounds
I'd never heard.

Oh Frank, she's singing Armenian
hymns and chants!
My mother turns and says to my dad
in her Boston accent

Riffing and singing anything
that came to mind—

but I know better now
there is ancient music
my child knows
sung off the cuff
in a '64 Chevy impala.

Migrations

just listen how desire
asks to come through

when the world is still arriving

dawn breaks through into morning

get out of the way, say YES

to a universe
waiting

to take shape

Pronouns of the World

my metatarsal, bottom of my foot unfurls
yoga toes
catch the ground
walking back and forth

as if every thought has a home
on the wood floor
on the wet earth, a walking prayer
an incantation of worry

is it prayer or worry?
thoughts of dear ones pulse
with repetition
if there could be a measure
all the pronouns of the world
would reach stars and constellations

these early morning ruminations
the house is still quiet, the cat
meows and wakes my thoughts

arise from sweat from the chasm of hormones
and prayers
water on my chest

how many times I pray
in the night for you
and you
and you.

Magic in the Pilaf

There is an Armenian saying,

Let even God think
you eat pilaf everyday

Rice Pilaf—a staple in our home
it was mandatory to have Uncle Ben's rice
as if he was Armenian himself

No other would do
as if it was organic and free-range

In the time of a pandemic, Uncle Ben's is nowhere
to be found
neither is toilet paper, flour and hand sanitizer

One starts with rice, what you did with it is what matters.
the ingredients you put in—

Sauté with onions, vermicelli, pine nuts then the rice.
Pour the boiling chicken broth and bring to boil again
simmer for twenty minutes

I thought there was some magic in the pilaf
a culture infused in grain
a pillar of resilience
making pilaf, the daily spiritual practice
feeding body and soul
a hint of the divine in each bite.

Illuminata

We are all illuminated
        walking manuscripts and womanscripts
etched khatchkars
        storied lives inscripted
        cellular memory beneath the skin.

We are scriptoria
writing our narratives
                co-creation.

Light cracks the wounds—

Here's a fact:
31,000 Armenian illuminated manuscripts
survive after invasions and massacres

Our hope is us
        we are the luminosity
of living parchment.

Offering

perhaps imagination
      is the final praise
            to look until we see

what offering beholds us
      in the mystery
            in the endless search

look beneath the surface
how many dimensions
      one object, one heart holds

in the company of light
look how radiance comes

sun circumferences
      the unseen and seen
      this too is a miracle
right in front of you.

Acknowledgements

Gratitude for the following publications, where some of these poems were first published in a previous form. Thanks to the following journals – *Ararat, Armenian Weekly, Toward the Light, The Armenite, Blue Skies, HyeBred,* and *Artisein: Arts & Teaching Journal.* Thanks to the book, *Identity landscapes: Contemplating place and construction of self,* and the blog, *Armenian Poetry Project,* where some of the poems were also published.

Thanks to Marsha Nouritza Odabashian who has been a collaborator and source of mutual inspiration. I am honoured to have her beautiful artistic images within this collection.

Thanks to those who have taken an interest in this manuscript and read or commented, or dialogued with me in the process, Tamar Haytayan, Lynn Fels, Michael Ling, Susan McCaslin, Dobee Snowber, Jackie Snowber and Anny St. Yves.

I am grateful for the ongoing conversations from my extended Armenian family and their support; Anna Demurjian, John and Garineh Goshdigian, Paula Terzian Harrop, Laura Terzian, John Terzian, Arpi Terzian, Mary Terzian, and Debbie Terzian.

Thanks to Kaija Pepper for our regular Café Calabria meetings on Commercial Drive where we supported one another's writing over the last several years.

I am thankful for the works of Peter Balakian, whose writing inspired me many years ago to keep forging my Armenian identity through the poetic. Thanks to the work of Lola Koundakjian whose dedication to the *Armenian Poetry Project* has been a beacon over the years.

Thanks to my editor Sylvia Taylor for her initial comments and encouragement.

Thanks to my poetry editor, Daniela Elza, who invited me to slice and cut into deeper beauty.

I want to heartily thank HARP Publishing the People's Press, Dorothy Lander and John Graham-Pole who are a delight and honour to work with. Their vision and enthusiasm for this book has meant the world to me.

Gratitude always to my sons, Lucas, Caleb and Micah for their love, exuberance and support of their mom.

And always, thanks to my beloved husband Shawn for his careful reading of my work and abiding love. He is clearly by now an Armenian by choice.

Photo Credit: Will Howcraft

Boston based artist and MFA, **Marsha Nouritza Odabashian's** drawings and paintings uniquely reflect the tension and expansiveness of being raised in dual cultures, Armenian and American. As a young child she watched her mother cultivate the Armenian tradition of dyeing eggs red by boiling them in onionskins. In her work, vignettes of current events, history and social justice emerge from the onionskin dye on paper, stretched canvas or compressed cellulose sponge. Her numerous solo exhibitions in the United States include *Skins* at the Armenian Museum of America in Watertown, *In the Shade of the Peacock*, *EXPUNGE* and *Miasma* at Galatea Fine Art in Boston. Group exhibitions include the Danforth Museum and Gallery Z. She has exhibited in Armenia twice: *New Illuminations* (HAYP Pop Up) and *Road Maps* (Honey Pump Gallery). Reviews of her work appear in *ArtScope*, *Art New England*, the *Boston Globe*, and the *Mirror Spectator*. Odabashian studies early and medieval Armenian art and architecture at Tufts University with Professor Christina Maranci, with whom she traveled to Aght'amar and Ani in Historic Armenia. Pairing her ancestral past with the present in her art is her means of fulfillment. She can be found at www.marshaodabashian.com.

Photo Credit: Michele Mateus

Celeste Nazeli Snowber, PhD is a dancer, poet, writer and award-winning educator who is a Professor in the Faculty of Education at Simon Fraser University outside Vancouver, B.C., Canada. Attention to embodied ways of inquiry has been central to Snowber's scholarly work for over two decades and she has pioneered dance and movement as a way of inquiry within the field of Arts-Based Research. She has published over fifty chapters and articles as well as six books. Among these are *Embodied prayer* and *Embodied inquiry: Writing, living and being through the body.* She has published her poetry widely and is author of two other collections of poems, *Wild tourist: Instructions to a wild tourist from the divine feminine* and co-author of *Blue Waiting.*

Celeste creates site-specific performances and has been the Artist in Residence in the University of British Columbia Botanical Garden creating full-length performances connecting poetry and dance out of each season. Celeste also creates one-woman shows integrating voice, comedy, and dance and has performed across North America and Internationally in a variety of venues, including concerts, galleries, museums, conferences and outdoor spaces. Celeste's mother was born in Historic Armenia in 1912 before immigrating to Boston and integral to Celeste's own artistic process is excavating fragments of ancestral memory, which find their way in poems and dances. Celeste is the mother of three amazing adult sons and lives outside Vancouver with her husband. She can be found at www.celestesnowber.com.